Partnership Promotion

Partnership Promotion

Table Of Contents

Table Of Contents	3
Introduction	4
What is a Joint Venture Partnership?	5
What's The Big Advantage?	6
The Single Most Vital Thing You Can Do	7
Other Tips To Consider	8
Top 8 Mistakes	9
The Fire Sale	10
Choosing Your Potential Partner	11
Where To Look	12
Finding Your First JV Partner	13
Why Warrior Forum?	17
Another Overlooked But Highly Effective Source Of JV Partner Leads	17
Starting Simply	18
"Do I Have To Try Their Product?"	19
What Traits Should You Look For In A JV Partner?	20
Researching Your Potential JV Partner	22
Building A Relationship	23
Building your relationship	25
Making Your Offer	26
Top Tips	28
Necessary Steps	28
2 Tools You Can Use	29
Dealing With Rejection	32
What To Do If There's No Reply	33
Letting Your List and Marketing Peers Know	33
Who Handles What	35

Introduction

You've probably read all sorts of posts and emails about the secrets of Joint Venture marketing. All of them offering up rosy visions that include you paired with the top Guru in your niche...

All of them claim it can easily happen... if you only do things the way they say.

It doesn't matter whether you approach a top guru or someone less prominent (with a large list!) Your success in landing *any* JV partner depends, like everything else in your marketing career, on:

- How driven you are
- How confident you are
- How creative you are
- How "lucky" you are
- How savvy and professional you are

But most of all, it depends on one other thing...

Knowing how to approach potential partners in a manner guaranteed to help them say "Yes."

And this report is going to help you do just that.

What is a Joint Venture Partnership?

Just so we're on the right page, let's quickly run through **how this works**...

In the world of internet marketing, a JV (or "joint venture") occurs when two separate internet marketers get together to promote one's product.

There many variations, but ultimately two basic types of Joint Venture, as understood in internet marketing:

- A partnership offer (both developing and launching the same product)
- A promotion-based offer (your JV partner promotes your product to his list)

In offline marketing, joint ventures are not taken lightly. These can take months to negotiate and a legal contract is always drawn up, with each party's responsibilities and rights laid out in black and white.

In internet marketing, however, there is usually no need for a contract unless you are actually developing a product together.

What's The Big Advantage?

The truth is, in internet marketing, a joint venture can be (and usually is) as simple as having a well-respected marketer in your niche provide a review or testimonial.

It can be as simple as sending an email to several marketers and having them say: "Okay, that looks like a win-win situation..."

Or it can indeed take several months, if you've opted for a partnership, and you and Marketer B are busy planning the Big Launch for a hot new product that will have both your names on.

If you're a new marketer, the simple promotional JV offer is by far the easiest to achieve. And it doesn't matter whether your potential JV partner is someone you simply found on Google, who you had never heard of before today – or the most staggeringly well-known marketer in your target niche:

Present your offer properly, and you'll make it easy for them to say: "Okay."

6 Questions To Ask Yourself Before You Approach them

1. "What risks and benefits can I anticipate?"
2. "What risks or benefits could my potential partner perceive?"
3. "What are my chances of making this a success?"

4. "How well have I researched the potential partner I want to approach?"

5. "Do I know how to give my JV proposal the best chance to succeed?"

6. "Will my product really benefit my potential partner's niche market?"

If your sole reason for this Joint Venture rests on being told you should do it, or getting a sudden idea, or making quick cash, you will definitely need to rethink it. These things may be true – but you may actually not be ready for a JV yet – or you may not know that there's one glaring condition guaranteed to make your JV offer flop on the spot.

So first, let's change that situation, before picking our marketer and crafting our offer...

The Single Most Vital Thing You Can Do

One thing you need to know – and do – up front. Without this condition being met, you won't have the slightest chance of attracting a JV partner.

Don't even *think* of proposing a JV venture until you have **your own Affiliate program completely set up and running**.

At the very <u>least</u>, take advantage of a third party Affiliate Marketplace network like Clickbank and pay the $50 one-time fee to list your product there. Clickbank will automatically set up an affiliate program for you, on that product. You'll have to follow their rules about commissions, payout and refunds. And you'll need to create a good Affiliate Center packed with resources specifically for you're your affiliates to use when promoting that product.

Not only will it help and please experienced affiliates, when they very properly write to you to see what resources you have to help them sell (or you let them know, in your JV offer)... it will enhance the professional image you are presenting to your potential JV partner.

Other Tips To Consider

One popular way to ensure a "yes": offer 100% commission to your potential JV partner. This tactic is a good one if you have a small list, and theirs is large. At this point, you're paying for the **exposure** and **web recognition** – as well as building your own list from sales she sends you (just make sure you know how to capture those leads without detracting from her commissions and captures.)

Also make sure that your own Affiliate script or service allows you to set cookies with a short expiry date. You may not intend to be giving your JV lifetime 100% commissions on every sale from that customer, right through your funnel – which is what will happen if you have "lifetime" cookies enabled.

And agree that the 100% is only for:

A. That product

B. The duration of the program

Top 8 Mistakes

There 8 things guaranteed not to incite a "Yes" answer, so make sure you've got them covered. The first one's so important, we're going to repeat it again:

1. Not having an affiliate program already set up
2. Not having all your affiliate resources complete, and ready to go for promotion
3. Approaching someone outside your narrow, specific niche
4. Not having a really strong and obvious USP (unique selling position)
5. Not having a strong and well-written offer
6. Expecting them to all the work
7. Not having any web visibility at all. (No social networking, no forum memberships, no favorite blogs where your comments are well known, etc.)
8. Not having any stats or conversion figures you can share with your potential JV partner

However, there's one more less obvious mistake that can really damage your reputation, if you don't know what you're doing…

One More Fatal Mistake Not To Make

9. Deciding you need a JV partner just to "make a quick buck".

JV partnerships should be about enhancing both your **reputations** and creating a trust-based relationship built for **longevity**.

However, if you honestly are more interested in "quick cash", but really need to power of a "bigger" marketer to get it, there is one popular solution you can initiate – or find, and jump on an already-started bandwagon….

The Fire Sale

You've seen these: You get an email from a marketer whose list you belong to, excitedly telling you about a "Blowout", with hundreds of free products by top name marketers. You go, and discover that you are able to download a pile of free eBooks (and the odd piece of software.)

In exchange, however, you have to sign up for each marketer's list.

The purpose of this exercise from all the marketers' point of view is a list-building exercise.

But it's a great opportunity for you to not only build your list, but get your name associated with well-known marketers – **if you have a high quality offering**.

One word of caution, however: You may be tempted to slap up any old thing. Don't do it! Make sure you over-deliver, and that the item you're contributed stands out like a beacon (it's your one chance to wow all the new people who sign up for your product, anyway.)

And remember that "qualifying" goes both ways: If the call for JV's for the fire sale is put out by marketers you consider sleazy or shady... or there are any other signs that they are going to rip people off with a bunch of ancient, already freely available old reports... don't touch them with a 10' pole.

It's not worth it, in the long run.

That being said, a fire sale with reputable marketers involved is a great way to either gain visibility and boost your list, or make some quick cash.

The way you do this: your free offer is dependent on one thing: the interested customer has to sign up to your list to receive his free product.

And here's your chance for an upsell, before he downloads his product.

Choosing Your Potential Partner

Here's what usually happens, when newer marketers start casting around for potential JV partners: They start thinking of the "Top Ten" names in their niche.

This is the wrong way to go about it.

Oh, you can just as easily land a big fish as one closer to you in experience and exposure… but think, first of all, about **the product you want to promote**. Answer your own list of questions about it – make one, and type it out, answers and all, if you're new to this (it's a great exercise and helps ingrain the correct thinking for future offers.)

1. Which specific niche is your product targeting?
2. Who is the exact customer who'll benefit most from it?
3. What makes it really unique and exciting for this niche?
4. What can it do for your exact customer? What benefit will it bring?
5. How will it make your exact customer's life better?
6. How much is he likely to be willing to pay?
7. How much am I selling it for?
8. How much can I afford to offer on commissions – and is it worth it, to build my list?

Where To Look

Rather than going through lists of potential marketers and trying to make your product "fit" their list, start with **the path of least resistance**.

You see, everyone turns the art of making JV offers into a big, scary monster, to be tiptoed round and feared – when nothing could be further from the truth! Your whole, ergonomic approach should be to "go with the flow"…

Because that's when true magic happens, when you allow your dream to "breathe". You're not trying to stuff it in some rigid little box, oblivious to the fact that it doesn't fit. Forcing something never works – ask Cinderella's Ugly Sisters.

Instead, start in the easiest place to look....

Finding Your First JV Partner

There is only one answer to the question "Where do I look for my ideal JV partner?" And the answer is: "Right within **your particular, unique niche**."

That's **Golden Rule # 1**.

But wait – don't go looking for the gurus just yet! What about that Mastermind group you belong to? Who runs it? Who do you talk to most often? Who have you built up a relationship with? Who do you feel comfortable with? Who do you trust? Whose list would be ideal candidates to benefit from for your product?

What about the Membership site you've been enjoying? Who runs it? Who do you talk to most often?...

Take a pen and paper (or your Text Editor; or whatever favorite writing program you prefer) and start making a list of all the places you suddenly realize you can look for a really well-targeted JV partner.

To help you out:

1. Mastermind Group
2. Membership Site
3. Twitter friends
4. Facebook or MySpace friends
5. Marketers whose blogs you comment on frequently, who know you by name
6. Affiliate marketers whose products you already promote (if you've never brought them a sale yet, scratch this source off the list!)
7. Forums you belong to – ones directly dealing with your specialty niche
8. Good old Google
9. Your competitors (yes, you heard that right)

Talk to your coach (you do have one, don't you?) Ask your buddies on the Mastermind group or Niche forum you belong to if they can suggest anyone – or if they're interested in being your JV partner. Tweet about it on Twitter. (It's usually done like this: "Looking for JV partner interested in helping me pioneer quiz-creator software. Please DM." DM in Twitterese stands for "direct message".)

If you are shaking your head, and telling me that you only belong to Facebook, you've got a lot of lost ground to cover! No one is going to want to JV with you if you have zero "web recognition", or web presence. They want to be able to say, "Oh yes. That's the woman who always posts those great wine tips.." or "Hmm, that's the great commenter who cracked me up last week with his pithy, intelligent comment."

You don't want them to sit there scratching there heads and saying: "Wanda *who*?"

If you don't yet have any web visibility at all, you're probably not ready for a JV partnership, in any way, shape or form. Your first step will be to **immediately** pick 5 highly relevant group venues, and spend at least a few weeks getting known by the people you want to approach. For the sake of convenience, let me suggest this highly effective smorgasbord:

- **Mastermind** group or **Membership** site relevant to your target niche
- The Warrior Forum
- **Active blog** by a (potential JV) marketer in your niche whose posts (and products you enjoy)
- The **affiliate blog** owned by the (potential JV) marketer whose goods you are currently promoting
- Twitter

Now get busy participating. Here's the way to do it gracefully:

- Introduce yourself on forums and group sites
- Post short, helpful comments, letting a smidgen of personality shine through
- Always remember to thank people for answers to your questions and concerns

And that's really all there is to practicing effective "web recognition".

Make your visit to your 4 or 5 venues **a regular part of your day**. Promise you'll do at least 2 Tweets on Twitter per day (be careful – it's addictive!) and answer 2 questions a day on every group site.

Space them out, if you like. Visit your Mastermind Group while you sip your morning coffee. Tweet at 12 noon, when you break for lunch. Read and comment your favorite marketer's latest blog post during your afternoon tea. Finish off after supper with Warrior Forum, or perhaps the Affiliate blog.

Why Warrior Forum?

If you're not familiar with WF, let me suggest it become a vital part of your marketing, if your category falls anywhere within the topics covered in its subsections. It's a great venue to test out your new product before its official launch – you can create a limited-time special offer in the Warrior Special Offer subsection (WSO). This allows other WF members to try out your product for a much-reduced price – and send you feedback and testimonials, which you'll gladly use, when you start to market your product (after tweaking it.)

The Warrior Forum members are a serious-minded bunch: A little intimidating, some people say – but you'll always get honest feedback, with no punches pulled. Which is worth its weight in gold!

Warrior Forum is free to join – and there is a Joint Venture section, where you can post JV offers or accept them.

Take heed of their warning, however: "If your first post is a JV offer, it will be deleted."

Another Overlooked But Highly Effective Source Of JV Partner Leads

Some of the best JV partnerships in history have occurred at **seminars, conferences and workshops.** Networking in person beats networking on line any day. Top freelancers have long known this secret source of contacts, and use it to connect with "high-end" clients.

If you have a high-ticket item, and want to attract big players, consider who goes to conferences all over North America – and sometimes abroad…

…It isn't the starving newbies.

It's also a good method to use if you want a true co-partnership, all the way from development to sales, rather than just a promotion boost.

Think of it: You and the normally-unapproachable top marketer are thrown together, you're both members (for the weekend, anyway) of the same, exclusive "club" – and if you really "click" on a personal level, you can form not just a profitable long-term JV partnership, but a life long business friendship.

But luckily for us mere mortals, this admittedly expensive approach is not usually necessary. Landing a JV partner really should be as simple as sending out a "Dear Joe" letter!

Starting Simply

One other overlooked method of finding a JV partner: Google them. (TIP: Look for those who give product reviews.)

It's very simple. Say you're product is an eBook on staying younger by looking after your skin the correct way…

Take your primary keyword for your product, and enter it in Google's search box like this:

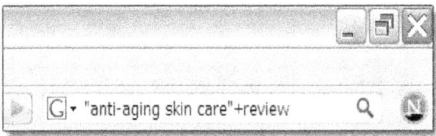

See who:

> ...has a list

> ...**reviews products**

> ...is a good fit with your niche market

Sign up for their newsletter and try out one of their products. Then approach them.

It really is as simple as that.

"Do I Have To Try Their Product?"

If you possibly can, and you're seriously considering them as a JV partner – well, yes! In fact, not only try their product, but sign up as an affiliate for it (as well as signing up for that newsletter.)

There's a really good reason.

If they're someone you don't yet know... someone you've picked off Google... it gives you a chance to see:

- How well they deliver
- If their own product is worthy of yours
- If your product is worthy of theirs
- How good their affiliate support is

As well as providing you with the opportunity to impress them with how actively you promote their product.

Of course, if you're approaching 20 marketers with JV requests, you don't have to do this for all of them.

But I'd really recommend it, if it's a "cold call" potential partner you don't know – one you've selected from Google.

What Traits Should You Look For In A JV Partner?

A seasoned marketer is going to be snorting with impatience, at this point. You'd hear them growling: "Hey, it's not rocket science. Just ask, already!"

And they're right. You'll be "just asking" too, before you know it.

But if you're new to the whole JV thing, it's a good idea to think things through, when you're familiarizing yourself with that territory.

One other mistake made by marketers new to joint ventures is seeking <u>out a partner who mirrors everything about themselves</u>. What makes great partnerships are not the similarities – it's the differences!

Of course, you don't want to be so different, you can't understand each other. But you don't want to be two peas in a pod, either.

You want a JV partner with specialties that compliment yours, not mimic them. Ideally, you'd like your partner to <u>compliment you in an area where you're weakest</u>.

For example, if you're great at writing information products, but a novice at marketing, one of the reasons you'll be picking that particular partner is because of his strong, proven sales skills.

If you absolutely hate doing videos and audio, and your partner loathes the written word – and you both have the same target market – you're a promotion team made in Heaven. Your partner can do the webinars and make videos; you can write blog posts and keep in touch with the forms.

A good way to figure out what you need in a partner: Analyze your own strengths and weaknesses.

Now, find a partner whose own strengths will compliment, rather than mirror, your specialty.

And yes – a direct competitor can serve this need quite well.

And now we've done our research, it's time to get things rolling...

Researching Your Potential JV Partner

Once you've chosen some likely JV partners as good candidates who might be genuinely interested in your offer, consider how you're going to approach them.

Your method should reflect how well you know them – and more importantly – how well they know **you.**

There is no hard and fast rule – though there are some conventions. However, you need to consider also how much of a stickler for convention your potential JV partner is likely to be.

You don't have to spend weeks researching your potential JV's. But even if you are approaching marketers you feel you know well, do invest in some in-depth but simple research on each one before you fire off that offer.

Stop and ask yourself... Have you:

1. Done a search for his sites and visited them?
2. Determined his target market?
3. Visited his blog and read all the comments?
4. Noted his writing style (does he use slang? does he swear? Is he very formal?)

5. Have you noted his age? (Say what you will: Age does affect your outlook and expectations of people in business.)

The simple truth is, people are flattered when you take the time to know what makes them tick.

Building A Relationship

One step well worth taking: Build a relationship with your marketer before you make a JV offer.

Let me reassure you - "building a relationship" in this case doesn't mean becoming his best friend in the whole wide world. It simply means making sure he has some recognition of your name, and feels connected to you in some small way.

At the very least, join his newsletter and stay on it for a few weeks before approaching him with your offer. Get to know him enough to confirm your initial impression that he'd make a good JV partner.

After all, whose proposal would **you** consider?

The marketer whose offer letter begins:

"*Dear Busy Marketer,*

I want YOU to promote my amazing new "Smack Chops" because it's an offer you'll really kick yourself in the butt over, if you're stupid enough to pass up this once in a lifetime get rich opportunity..."

Or the one whose offer letter begins:

"Dear Jennifer,

I've been enjoying your newsletter since discovering it on your website, BigSite.com. My interest was hooked by your E-Z Recipe Selector. Since I have a really busy lifestyle and it sounded as if it would solve my "too-tired-to-cook" dilemma, I purchased it and found it not only saved me hours of time, but was fun to use...'

Of course, if you're a SmackChops kinda guy, and so is the potential JV you're approaching, there's a chance the former approach might work (but **don't** call him "Dear Busy Marketer", no matter what everyone else does nowadays.)

This example also gives you a Sneak Peek at another solid tip: Tailor your offer to your potential JV partner's style.

Another Plus To Have In Your Ball Court

One of the best things you can do for yourself: Already be an affiliate for your JV.

Only you'd better not be the sort of affiliate that just sticks a link on their site and makes no further effort to promote. It goes without saying that marketers naturally look more favorably on the affiliate who has been busting her buns to land them sales – whose efforts they've noticed.

That being said, all the affiliate sales in the worlds are barely going to buy you two seconds, if you don't present a professional, irresistible proposal that promises great benefits, almost no work on your Marketer's part and a clear and obvious benefit to her list.

Building your relationship

We'll make this simple: 6 proven ways of building a relationship…

1. Join his membership site. Not just so you can cozy up to him about a future joint venture, but more importantly, so you can get to know the sort of people represent his top, lifelong recurring customers. You need to make sure they're a fit for purchasing your products as he is, selling it!

2. **Sign up for her Webinar or Teleseminar** and participate actively, with relevancy. Afterwards, write a simple email thanking her for her time and letting her know one or two points of interest you found particularly found valuable. (Everybody likes feedback – and testimonials.)

3. **Write a review** of one of his products, then email him to let them know him know his product was the subject of your post. Give him the post link, but absolutely don't even hint at any possible JV partnership, at this point. This is just to bring yourself onto his radar, until you've

established a relationship. (No, it's not as quick a strategy as just mailing a letter – but this is a good investment if you're looking at **long-term** cooperation and repeated partnerships with your marketer.)

4. **If she has a Mastermind site, join it**. If it has an "inner circle", join that too. It may be the best investment you ever make.

Making Your Offer

Remember, this is not some big, scary deal you have to take months to work your courage up to tackle. Sure, you've taken half an hour to research him on the net; and sure, signed up for her newsletter and hung out on her forum for a couple of weeks. But that should have been something you fitted easily into your schedule.

But now you've signed up with Clickbank, got your Affiliate Center pre-loaded with tutorials, banner ads, text ads, and any other marketing tools your JV partner can just pick up and use.

You're ready to make the offer.

There are two simple ways to do it:

1. **Contact the marketer of your choice and let him that you're about to launch a new product**. Tell him why you really value his opinion – perhaps give *him* a testimonial about one of his products. Ask if he'd be interested in taking a look at your product, and give you his honest opinion.

   At this point, you can go ahead and continue to make this a formal JV offer... or you can simply ask if he'll review your product (hoping he will, and then send you back a letter saying: "How can I help you sell it?" or "I think my list could really benefit from your product, why don't we...")

   If you're shy, just asking for a review is an option you may feel more comfortable with. But at this point, **there's really no reason not to be straightforward**, and just make an offer anyway.

   (Besides, if he does simply review your product, and offers nothing more... that's already s a simple form of Joint Venture partnership in itself!

   His list will read his review. It will rank well on Google.

   And you'll have many new customers and subscribers, in no time at all.)

2. **Simply pick up the phone and call**. This one works best, of course, if you already have the sort of relationship where you feel comfortable enough to phone. If you've never phoned your JV prospect before, you may want to consider another method. But if you've exchanged Skype calls over various issues, a time or two... or you've ever had any coaching sessions with him... the telephone can be a great time-saver.

Top Tips

Be sure to include your Skype number along with your signature, so he will know (a) he can call you for free (b) you're a pro who knows all the right tools to use – it's amazing how many marketers don't even know about Skype: Much less actually use it. (Free calling: just one more small incentive to make it easy for him to pick up the phone...)

Necessary Steps

If you're approaching a top-level marketers, be aware that many won't even look at an offer unless it's a **high ticket item**, with a hefty price tag and commission.

If yours isn't, consider a marketer closer to your peer level

2 Tools You Can Use

Finally, here are two helpful worksheets you can print out, as many times as you like. Start filling the first one out as soon as you begin to research your potential partner, so you've got all the facts at your fingertips

The second one will be helpful when you're crafting the offer itself.**Potential JV Partner**	
My Product Name:	
Date:	
Potential JV Partner's Name:	
Phone/Skype Number:	
Email:	
Website:	
Newsletter?	☐ Yes ☐ No (couldn't find one)
Newsletter Site Address:	
Niche Segment	
His/Her USP:	
Why he/she would make good partner	

choice:	
What I liked about his/her product or site:	
How my product relates to his/her list:	
Benefits of my product:	

My Offer Details	
My Product Name:	
Date:	
Potential JV Partner's Name:	
Phone/Skype Number:	
Email:	
Website:	

Newsletter:	
Commission details:	
Bonuses I can offer:	
Partnership or promotion?	
What do I want them to do? (Review? Provide Bonus? Testimonial? Etc.)	
What I can give their customers:	
Affiliate Link set up for them:	
How/when they'll get paid	
My Conversion Stats for this product :	
Download link for this product:	

Dealing With Rejection

You've invested all that time and energy – and all your potential Joint Venture partners turned you down! You can't help feeling disappointed and defeated.

This is entirely normal – but it might help if you remember one thing: Their reasons for turning you down may have nothing to do with you personally. In fact, I can think of 6 really valid reasons, right off the top of my head...

1. They've just signed a JV offer for a similar product
2. Their schedule is loaded to the max for the better part of the year
3. They may actually be just about to change their marketing focus
4. They may be winding down, preparing to `retire'
5. They may just not think it's a good fit for their niche
6. They may have decided generally that JV partnerships don't work for them

The worst mistake you can make at this point is to assume that door is forever closed. I know of 3 people who were initially turned down, who ended up working with their respective potential partners further down the road (very successfully!)

Send the marketer your best "Thank You" letter – after all, he took the time to read your proposal (you hope!) (Give him the benefit of the doubt.) – and move on, for now.

Look to see if there is anything about your proposal you can improve, before sending it on to your next prospect.)

What To Do If There's No Reply

It's a big mistake to take silence as a "no". Spam filters may have gobbled up your letter – or their inbox could have been so flooded that day, they didn't even notice it among all their other JV offers.

Or they just may be very busy, and haven't had time to even look at it yet.

Your best bet is to wait at least one week, then send them a short, straightforward email.

You're not "bugging" them - and many a JV has occurred after an undaunted marketer took this simple, correct follow-up step.

However, if you still don't hear back, don't bombard them with emails. Just move on.

Letting Your List and Marketing Peers Know

You've finally landed that JV partner! How do you let the world know without bouncing up and down like an excited Chihuahua?

Well, the truth is, if bouncing up and down like an excited Chihuahua suits your personality and niche, go ahead and bounce. But most people will prefer to promote their new contact in a more civilized but no less enthusiastic manner.

Let me point out a wonderful advantages you can leverage right away, before we get into details…If your partnership is only for 3 weeks after the launch (because he's off to Patagonia), say, you can use this short time-frame to create that much-desired "sense of urgency" about your offer.

Meanwhile…

- Let your list know
- Create a website for the new project and announce it (remember, as the "junior" partner who did the approaching, you'll likely have wooed your partner by doing most of the work)
- Blog about it – and also get yourself from guest posts, announcing your new partnership there (in a manner relevant to your post, of course.)
- Let your affiliates know in a separate email (or the next edition of your affiliate newsletter, if it's about to come out.)
- Consider a short PPC campaign, just to announce the launch
- Build anticipation by counting down the days. Give away "pre-launch" prizes for early signup to be notified

- Contact web Radio shows, and see if you can be a special guest. Don't talk about your promotion – offer to talk about the subject it is related to. The radio host knows the score, and most likely will allow you to plug your project at the beginning and end of the clip
- Take out ads in relevant eZines (they're a lot cheaper than "regular" ads)

Who Handles What

There's an easy answer to that one: As the person soliciting the JV, be prepared to do 90% of the work before approaching your marketer. (Golden Rule # 2: **Remove all obstacles. Make it harder to say "no" than "yes" to your JV offer.**)

Also, you'll both naturally play to your strengths (especially in a partnership type of venture.)

There will always be "grey" areas. Try to anticipate them and make a list of what needs covering. Go over any "grey" areas with your JV partner, to make sure you're both on the same track with who is going to do what.

And remember – if things go harmoniously, this may be the first step of a recurring JV relationship you'll both benefit from and enjoy for a long time to come.

www.ingramcontent.com/pod-product-compliance
Lightning Source LLC
LaVergne TN
LVHW020502080526
838202LV00057B/6109